Original title:
The Plant Parent Diaries

Copyright © 2025 Creative Arts Management OÜ
All rights reserved.

Author: Harris Montgomery
ISBN HARDBACK: 978-1-80581-785-7
ISBN PAPERBACK: 978-1-80581-312-5
ISBN EBOOK: 978-1-80581-785-7

A Garden's Whisper

In pots they sit, our leafy friends,
Each day we water, just to pretend.
A secret club of green delight,
They gossip plants by chilly night.

With tangled roots and leaves askew,
I swear they plot, these greens adieu.
'Water me more!' they seem to plead,
Yet feast on sunlight, that's their greed.

Oh, how they thrive, while I just sigh,
For if they could, they'd wave goodbye.
I'll talk to them, they'll nod and sway,
Still, growing hands will steal my day!

In morning light, they stretch and yawn,
While I just sip my coffee—gone!
They laugh at me, how silly I look,
As I study them like an open book.

Green Tendrils of Devotion

In my kitchen, a jungle grows,
Pothos fights for the light, who knows?
A cactus whispers, 'Don't touch me!'
While the ferns just laugh, wild and free.

Spilling soil, oh what a sight,
My plant friends party late at night.
With sips of water, they toast to health,
I swear they're plotting against my wealth.

Soil Secrets and Sunlight Dreams

Need to prune, but where's my graft?
In the mess, I lose my craft.
Hands dirty, potting mix on my face,
Pest control's like a wild chase.

Sunlight streams in, plants start to dance,
Do they know how to sing or prance?
In their little pots, secrets unfold,
As they tell stories of sunlight bold.

A Garden of Heartbeats

In my abode, a heartbeat hums,
Plants speak softly, 'We want crumbs!'
With every leaf and with every sprout,
They giggle and whisper, no room for doubt.

Once a wilt, now a proud green sage,
Chasing away all the green envy rage.
They cheer me up, it's quite the show,
As I dance through the leaves, don't let them grow!

Cultivating Companionship

My succulents like to huddle tight,
Sharing gossip under soft starlight.
'Who needs friends when you've got thyme?'
'And don't forget mint, it's so sublime!'

Snake plants give the best advice,
'Just stand tall; life's a little spice!'
I'm the jester, they're the kings,
In this quirky court, laughter springs.

Little Green Stories

Watering at dawn, what a sight,
My pants soaked through, oh what a plight!
Dancing plants sway, full of glee,
While I trip on roots, oh woe is me!

Fertilizer fumes swirl in the air,
My cat sneezes loud, gives me a scare.
Cacti don't need hugs, I learned the hard way,
But they still seem to glare, 'Please go away!'

Echoes of the Earth

My little sprouts shout, 'Give us some light!'
But the sun's on vacation, oh what a fright.
The broccoli's plotting, it whispers to me,
'Why'd you plant me next to that giddy radish tree?'

A garden ghost whispers, 'Water with cheer!'
But spills my drink—now there's no beer!
The lettuce giggles, 'What a wild date!'
I respond, 'At least I'm not eating my fate!'

The Caregiver's Garden

In my jungle of pots, where the chaos is rife,
Plants argue daily, debating their life.
The ferns are gossiping, oh what a crew,
While I'm tangled in vines, feeling like stew!

A rogue tomato rolled down the path,
I couldn't help but laugh at its wrath.
With a wink from the basil, my heart's full of cheer,
Tending to plants is just like a beer!

Whimsical Woods

The snarky ferns mock my pruning style,
As I wrestle with twigs, they wink and smile.
The mint's on a mission, plotting to spread,
While I'm left wondering which flower is dead.

A squirrel swoops in, stealing my snacks,
While the daisies giggle, 'Watch out for attacks!'
Nature's a circus of laughs and surprise,
In my quirky green world, joy never dies!

Blossoms and Bonding

I watered my fern, what a splash!
It turned into a mini water crash.
The cat looked on with eyes so wide,
Wondering if I had lost my pride.

Joy blooms through mischief and grace,
Green monsters smile upon my face.
I pruned a leaf, thought I was slick,
But now it's just a sad green stick.

In the Company of Green

A cactus perched upon my desk,
Whispered secrets, truly grotesque.
Its needles pricked my curious hand,
A prickly friendship, quite unplanned.

Ferns and succulents join the crew,
They gossip wildly when I'm not due.
In this green world, I'm the jester,
Tripping over pots, oh my, what a tester!

Green Thumb Chronicles

Watering one day, I lost my way,
My plant said, "Hey, can we play?"
I turned to see its leafy grin,
My gardening skills were wearing thin.

Potted pals on the window sill,
They sway and dance, oh what a thrill!
But not one has ever told me,
Why my herbs like to play hide and seek!

Leaves of Love

I tried to sing to my variegated plant,
It wilted, and I thought, "What a gallant!"
My serenade must have been too loud,
Or perhaps it thought I was too proud.

Oh, what joy in this leafy affair,
My plants keep secrets; they don't seem to care.
With every leaf and every sprout,
My garden thrives—there's no doubt!

Nurturing Soil Stories

Oh dear, another leaf dropped,
It's clearly not my fault!
I swear I watered them,
But perhaps not as they'd like.

Fertilizer? A little too much,
Now they're swaying like they dance!
I tried to teach them manners,
Yet they just want to prance.

Root rot on a Wednesday night,
What a twist in my tale!
They wiggle in the soil,
Challenging my gardening scale.

Talking to my plants is great,
Except when they talk back!
With sass and a growth spurt,
I knew I'd be under attack.

Whispers of the Wilderness

In the jungle of my living room,
The ferns are starting to plot.
Potted plants with gossip,
Who knew they had such a lot?

Cacti stand proud and alone,
But they're judging my çdo hand,
Saying, 'You call this watering?'
As I spill beer in the sand.

Herbs argue with the violets,
'We're fragrant, can't you smell?'
While succulents roll their eyes,
In this weird green hotel.

All the soil critters whisper,
'This garden's got no peace!'
But I'd call it quite chaotic,
Funny though, never a cease!

Tendrils of Time

Time flies when plants are near,
Though mine don't seem to grow.
Each tick feels like a year,
What's wrong? I just don't know!

Yesterday they begged for sun,
Today, they crave the rain.
Its like they've got a plan,
Or maybe they're just insane?

Measuring moisture is the game,
Yet they thrive on neglect!
I tried a fancy chart,
But they chose to reject.

With tendrils so mischievous,
They reach for what they can steal,
Taking snacks off of my plate,
A plant's a sneaky deal!

Botanica's Secret Journal

Between the leaves and pots,
Lies a journal with a twist.
Entries filled with silly notes,
Of the plants that I resist.

'Dear reader, I must confess,
The spider plant's a spy!
It watches all my secrets,
And I can't figure why.'

'Today the orchids plotted,
To steal my last piece of cake.
While snake plant tried to charm me,
I'm wise to its fun fake!'

Oh, the tales that plants would tell,
If only they could speak.
Yet through their leaves I see,
A bond so strong, unique.

The Essence of Evergreen

In a pot, my green friend sits,
Loving sunlight, but hates the drips.
I water him like he's a pet,
Yet he still gives me a reason to sweat.

Leaves that curl and turn all brown,
I tried to smile, but then I frown.
He's staging a slow-motion fight,
And I'm losing, oh what a plight!

Fertilize on a Tuesday morn,
Screaming 'You're fine!', a plant forlorn.
He stares back like a silent foe,
Why can't he just grow and glow?

Expecting blooms, I'm out of luck,
My plant is nothing but a stubborn muck.
Yet here we are, a silly pair,
Laughing at life in my little lair.

Tending to Time

I set reminders on my phone,
To check on Herb all alone.
But days go by, he's still the same,
A stoic warrior in this game.

I talk to him of dreams and fate,
He listens well, but won't relate.
A sage who offers zero tips,
But greets me back with leafy quips.

Too much water, the roots do complain,
A drought, and he looks half insane.
Oh dear Herb, can't you see?
Our bond's too tangled, just let it be!

With time, I learn the dance we share,
I whisper, "Grow," he just gives a glare.
Yet every day, I give it a shot,
This journey of growth, what a funny knot!

Joy in the Jungle

In corners bright, my jungle thrives,
A mishmash of greens, and no one drives.
A funky fern with frizzy hair,
And a cactus that dreams of the fair.

I trip on pots, they're everywhere,
A quick dance moves with lots of flair.
They giggle as I make a mess,
In my little zoo, what a cute stress!

Mischief blooms with every sprout,
Sass and sassafras, they shout.
"Leaf me alone," my poor petunia sighs,
While the napkin plant gives me big, wide eyes.

Yet through the chaos, love does grow,
In this wild kingdom, we steal the show.
I wouldn't trade a single leaf,
For the joy in this jungle of disbelief!

Nature's Nurturing Notebook

I jot down notes, my gardening lore,
"Water on Tuesday, and clothes on the floor!"
A blunder here, a giggle there,
My green thumb's turning quite rare.

Checklists sprawling, my notes a mess,
Yelling, "How hard could it be to impress?"
Yet here I am learning on the spot,
My leafy friends think I'm a putz, quite a lot.

"More sunlight!" I shout at the shade,
As my herb's hiding, just not afraid.
A testament to each tangled vine,
Who knew tending could be such a line?

Yet each faded plant tells a tale,
With memories of laughter, where some fail.
In nature's notebook, I find my glee,
Growing with humor, it's just us three!

Sprouts of Serenity

My fern just did a pirouette,
Watering can's now a threat.
Cactus pricks my dreams at night,
I can't tell if it's out of spite.

My aloe's got a wicked grin,
Counting all the times I've sinned.
Basil's plotting with the mint,
Saying I should give a hint.

In Leafy Embrace

Bonsai shimmies in its pot,
Asking if I've really thought.
That spider plant glares with sass,
Saying my care could use a pass.

Of course my succulents are fine,
Except when it's too much sunshine.
Fern's all tangled in the mess,
My cat thinks it's a game of chess.

Flourishing Together

My peace lily waves hello,
"Did you forget? It's time to grow!"
The pothos climbs with sharp intent,
Plotting where my snacks are spent.

The jade plant's on a diet spree,
Every leaf's a mystery.
I'm convinced the thyme's a spy,
Sniffing out my cooking lie.

Sanctuary of Seeds

In my pot, a riot brews,
Promising it won't snooze.
Mint leaves scheming, citrus dreams,
Growing wild with laughing beams.

Tomatoes giggle in their row,
Daring me to steal the show.
Herbs are whispering, plotting worlds,
In this chaos, green joy swirls.

Cultivated Dreams

I dream of greens sprouting high,
In a jungle made of pots nearby.
Yet half my plants are hanging low,
I watered them too much, oh no!

Succulents wink with a cheeky grin,
They thrive despite where I've been.
Herbs laugh as I cut off a leaf,
A salad bowl now brings me grief!

My cacti wear their spikes with pride,
But only one stands by my side.
I tried to share the love around,
In plant and chaos, I almost drowned!

Night falls and I sigh with delight,
I hope they don't hold me too tight.
In this green chaos, pure and bright,
I find joy, come morning light.

Growing Pains and Gains

Oh, these seedlings really have the knack,
To grow straight up, then take a crack.
I swore I'd give them perfect care,
But they drooped low, in pure despair!

The fern yells "More light!" with a flutter,
While spider plants spin, causing clutter.
Each watering can feels like a game,
I scream a name; they're all the same!

A neighbor's pet made a snack of my thyme,
But I laugh it off, it's just plant crime.
I pot my dreams and hope for blooms,
As soil fights back from those tiny looms.

With every sprout comes joy and woe,
A botanical circus, this I know.
Yet the laughter echoes in my space,
I'm a plant parent with a silly face!

Flora and Family

In my home, a green family thrives,
More leafy faces than I have lives.
My dog stares at the ivy like kin,
Can plants help with all that fur and din?

The kids run wild, they skip and scream,
While my herbs plot an aromatic dream.
When they spill dirt in a fit of glee,
I can't help but chuckle, oh, let it be!

Grandpa says they talk back sometimes,
He's convinced they sing silly rhymes.
The ferns, he claims, express their views,
While the geraniums all wear shoes!

In this household of flora and cheer,
I'm a jester in a garden sphere.
With love and laughter, we all grow wide,
In this wild wonder, I take such pride.

The Garden of Gratitude

In my garden of thankfulness, oh what fun,
Where marigolds dance and the sun is spun.
With each petal I give a heartfelt cheer,
For mess and sunshine, I hold so dear.

I learned my lessons from leaf to stem,
With each mishap, I write a gem.
Dancing worms and the buzzing bees,
Bring laughter louder than summer breeze.

While watering can spills like a flood,
And flowers fight back, creating mud,
I find myself giggling more each day,
In this garden mischief, joy finds a way.

So let's toast to green, to roots and to leaves,
To every errant sprout, let's take our leaves!
In this garden brimming with light and glee,
My heart's the happiest it can be!

The Petals of Patience

Water, water, where are you?
I swear I just filled the cup, it's true!
Each leaf sighs, a silent plea,
As I debate with my adulting spree.

I checked the soil, gave it a poke,
Is that a root or just a joke?
My peace lily grimaced, rather abrupt,
While my cactus laughed – it's always tough.

Sunshine streamed through the window pane,
But my fern decided to play insane.
A moody plant, a diva indeed,
Can't find a line from the garden creed.

One day I'll thrive, just wait and see,
With plant-care tips from TikTok, maybe!
But for now, I'll just sit and tease,
My leafy pals with a glass of ease.

Secrets of the Succulent

In my care, they seem so shy,
These prickly friends, oh me, oh my!
I watered one, now it's looking swell,
But the others staged a protest bell.

One named Spike, oh such a tease,
Winks at me with his spiny ease.
I told him jokes, but no reaction,
Just a slow grow – such a fraction!

I tried to hug the furry ones,
They poked me back – what silly puns!
A rose in fact is quite polite,
Too bad it just won't take a bite.

Oh secret friends that brightly gleam,
Chasing sunlight, living the dream.
With humor and love, I'm in the zone,
A plant-parent never alone!

Verdant Reflections

In the mirror I see green glee,
A jungle kingdom, fair and free.
Leaves whisper with a joking tone,
'Water us now or we'll be grown!'

Each morning starts, a dance with light,
I juggle pots with all my might.
A cactus grins—oh, what a sight,
I step back, avoiding a fight!

My herbal friends, they love to tease,
One leaf flutters like a breeze.
While I shake my head, rolling my eyes,
Do they hold meetings? Oh, what a surprise!

With laughter filling up the room,
I promise to chase away the gloom.
They're more than just plants, they're friends divine,
In my green house, I still feel fine!

Sowing Seeds of Kindness

I planted friendship in a pot,
Watered it daily, gave it a shot.
Yet weeds crept in, oh not again!
They say, "Don't feed them!" Oh what a pain.

Each sprout needs love, a sprinkle or two,
But will they thrive? Who knew that's true?
A herb that's bitter, another that's sweet,
Mix them all and voila! A treat!

Seeds of laughter, growing in rows,
Share a smile and it always shows.
Blossoms and giggles, the best of blends,
In my garden, we're all friends!

With tender care, I plant each thought,
Nurtured with humor, never forgot.
From tiny sprouts to a verdant spree,
The joy of gardening sets us free!

The Language of Leaves

Whispers of green on every stem,
Telling tales of my watering gem.
They're judging my habits, oh what a sight,
Frowning when I forget to give light.

A leaf droops low, is it thirst or a tease?
I panic and pour, they're just playing, with ease.
Sassy little monsters, they twist and they bend,
In this leafy dialogue, will it ever end?

Love in a Terracotta Home

In a pot of brown, my heart starts to swell,
With plants that I treat as if under a spell.
Terracotta dreams filled with soil and some jokes,
Chatting with cacti, aren't they just folks?

The fern's got a flair, it's quite the charmer,
But it shushes me if I sound like a farmer.
Romancing my succulents with water and care,
Yet one decided to grow, just to beware.

Between Watering and Worrying

A dance of despair when the leaves start to droop,
I check all their roots, am I losing my troop?
Fingers crossed tight, with a light heart I pray,
Maybe they like it when I go away?

I drown them in love, but they seem to float by,
Flirting with death, as I start to cry.
In this life of drama, I try not to grieve,
Finding solace in blooms, oh what a reprieve!

Seasons of Green: Chronicles of Care

Winter brings chill, and they sigh with a freeze,
While I ponder if they've all caught a disease.
Spring blossoms bright, and we dance through the day,
Nature's own soap opera—come watch, come play!

Summer's heat hits, and my water rules break,
They soak up the sun, leaving me quite awake.
Fall brings the drama, with leaves that descend,
Writing tales of green, I hope they don't end!

Harvesting Happiness

I plant with hope and with delight,
Each tiny seed, a future bright.
Yet weeds, they laugh, they sprout so bold,
In my garden tales, their stories told.

My watering can, a trusty friend,
Its silver spout, where laughter blends.
I splash and drench, they wave back cheer,
These leafy fools bring me good cheer.

From thorns of doubt, I tend to rise,
A sprout of joy in every surprise.
Lettuce may wilt, but I'll still wear a grin,
For every green leaf, there's always a win.

The Joy of Roots

In the soil, roots twist and twirl,
Like dancers in a leafy whirl.
I tiptoe close, with a knowing grin,
Their jokes are earthy, always begin!

Potatoes hide beneath the earth,
They giggle and chuckle, oh what mirth!
'Plant me deep!' they holler with flair,
As I dig up treasures without a care.

Radishes peep from their cozy beds,
With tops like hair, they play at threads.
'Look at me!' they cry, so proud and spry,
With roots like jokes, they'll make you sigh.

A Symphony in Green

In my garden, a concert brews,
With crickets chirping their nightly blues.
Each leaf a note, each bloom a song,
Nature's orchestra, where I belong.

Tomatoes sway in blazing light,
'Catch me if you can!' they tease with might.
While basil hums a fragrant tune,
In this green symphony, all is in bloom.

The sun waves hello, the moon gives a wink,
Together they dance while I sit and think.
These little laughs and garden quirks,
Fill my heart with joyful perks.

Flourish of the Heart

Oh, my dear ferns, so plush and grand,
With fronds that wave like a quirky band.
They lean and stretch in playful glee,
'Join us, friend, come dance with me!'

Succulents sit with a smug little grace,
In their plumpness, they find their space.
'Water us less, we like it dry!'
They smirk at me, as I sigh and comply.

Inhaling scents of mint and thyme,
In this jumble of green, I find my rhyme.
Each silly sprout, a story to start,
In a garden full of laughter, I flourish my heart.

Blooming Together

My succulents are in a race,
To see who drinks the most in place.
I swear they know how to conspire,
Plotting green plots that never tire.

The fern whispers secrets late at night,
While the cactus pricks with all its might.
My watering can's now a magic wand,
Ensuring my plants form a happy band.

The Gardener's Heart

I thought I'd just try some thyme,
But now I'm lost in herbal rhyme.
Basil dreams of a sunny spree,
While mint insists it's living free.

My heart's entwined with leafy greens,
As I decipher their leafy scenes.
Every day's a new green quest,
A battle between bloom and jest.

Fruition and Flourish

Tomatoes tango in the sun,
As peppers play, oh what a fun!
My veggies dance in rows so neat,
While I trip over them, oh what a feat!

The carrots giggle underground,
In their orange coats, they're so renowned.
Zucchini rolls, trying to hide,
While I with laughter, won't abide.

Nature's Nurturers

The daisies gossip, oh so sweet,
While daisies plot my gardening feat.
My hands in dirt, I laugh and play,
Who knew plants could brighten my day?

The ivy climbs to reach my dreams,
But tangles me in its leafy schemes.
I'm a keeper of all things green,
In a world where laughter reigns supreme.

Verdant Ventures

I bought a cactus, oh what a buy,
He barely needs water, just a wink and a sigh.
My coworkers think I'm a gardening star,
But really, it's green, no need for flair by far.

Succulents smile while I'm sweating in doubt,
A fern on my desk whispers, 'You need a sprout!'
I talk to them daily, have they heard my plight?
Guess I'm just a plant whisperer, day and night.

The spider plant's webbed, a tangled affair,
My skills are a joke, but I act like I care.
The philodendron says, 'Grow me if you can!'
I just nod along, hiding my secret plan.

In the jungles of home, I graciously roam,
Plant fever's taken me far from my tome.
With pots on the counter and soil on the floor,
I'm just a green thumb, forever wanting more!

The Soil Beneath

Digging in dirt, I feel like a king,
But every time I sneeze, it's a dust storm fling.
Worms wiggle past as I dance on the ground,
Each shovel of earth is a treasure I've found.

My lovely friends, they roll their wide eyes,
As I talk about mulch like it's some grand prize.
They say, 'You're crazy!' with voices sincere,
But what do they know? Gardening's full of cheer!

A ladybug landed, and I gave a salute,
'Your wings are so cool in this leafy pursuit!'
They chuckled and laughed at my soil-filled delight,
But little do they know, I'm living the life!

Days spent repotting, oh what a thrill,
I chat with my plants, hear them laugh and shrill.
The roots seek adventure, while I hum a tune,
Embracing the chaos beneath the green moon.

Blossoms of Belonging

A bouquet of petals, my heart feels so light,
They sway in the breezes, a colorful sight.
From daisies to tulips, I fill up my space,
With floral companions, there's joy in each place.

At the market, I stumble, my cart starts to tilt,
With flowers and leaves, I'm growing my quilt.
'Can we fit one more?' I ask in a rush,
They giggle and nod, 'You must love this lush!'

In the corner of home, the orchids convene,
They whisper sweet secrets, it's a plant parent dream.
I give them a drink, and they blush with delight,
We share all our stories deep into the night.

A neighbor walks by, shakes her head with a grin,
'You have enough blooms, now let's reel it in.'
But flowers are laughter, and laughter's a must,
In this world full of petals, just know it's a plus!

Growing with Grace

With watering can ready, I stride like a queen,
In the realm of my plants, I'm the brightest green.
They cheer as I sprinkle, a shower of love,
While plotting world takeover, like ants from above.

My rubber plant's stretching, it dreams of the sky,
While succulents giggle, with twinkles in eye.
Each leaf tells a story, of loam and of light,
But I swear on my soil, they're planning my fright.

Little seedlings peek as I whisper my hopes,
They snicker and wiggle, they have grand scopes.
Imitating dances, they sway with the tune,
My house now a garden, a wild green festoon.

As I trip on my rope, I'm caught in the fray,
Each pot's a companion, come join the ballet!
With laughs and with blooms, life's delightfully wild,
In the garden of laughter, I'm nature's own child.

Serene Sprouts

In a pot beside the sink, they dwell,
Little green friends, each with a story to tell.
One's a bit saucy, thinks he's the king,
Waving his leaves, oh, what joy they bring!

Water? No! Just a talk and some light,
Chat with my ferns — they're quite the delight.
Forget the fertilizer, it's gossip and cheer,
I swear they grow faster when I'm near!

A cactus near the stove, prickly and proud,
Claims he's the best, says it out loud.
But give him too much love, and he'll hiss,
"Just a quick hug, not a plant parent kiss!"

So here in my jungle, we laugh and we play,
Each sprout has its quirks, brightening the day.
With leaves that sway to our whimsical tunes,
In our green little world, we're all happy goons.

Roots of Resilience

Oh, my roots dig deep in this messy old pot,
They've seen things, you know, that most don't allot.
Dirt on my shirt? Nah, it's a badge of pride,
Each spill is a story, let the wildness guide!

Last week, I tried yoga, a stretch and a pose,
But I tripped on my fern, she started to doze.
Now they say I'm clumsy, but I prefer free,
It's just my plants enjoying a laugh at me!

A sprout sighed, "Chill, we still love this mess!"
"Life's a bit crazy, but isn't it blessed?"
With a nod, I agree, as the sun hits their leaves,
Roots weaving laughter, like autumnal eaves.

So here we grow stronger, in sunlight and shade,
These quirky companions, our memories made.
With roots wrapped in laughter, we thrive side by side,
In the pot of resilience, joy cannot hide.

Blossoms and Bonds

In this snazzy abode with blossoms galore,
Life's all sunshine, with blooms to explore.
One's a diva, demands all the light,
While another pretends it's a star in the night!

Each morning's a show, they preen and they pose,
With petals a-dancing, in hues like a rose.
A sunflower grinning from the window's wide view,
Proudly declares, "I outshine the crew!"

We've got our disagreements, like who gets the chair,
But through ups and downs, there's plenty to share.
With laughter and love, we've formed a tight crew,
In the comedy of growth, we're all blooming too!

So here's to my blossoms, each petal and stem,
Through giggles and gaffes, we're one happy gem.
With bonds made of joy, we'll bloom till the end,
In this vibrant oasis, where all laughs transcend.

Ferns in the Family

In a corner they gather, the ferns in a row,
Swaying like dancers, putting on quite the show.
One's got a frizzle, thinks he's quite chic,
While the others just giggle, with roots kind of meek!

A fight over sunlight, oh what a sight,
"Mind your own leaves!" one will quip in delight.
I pour out some water and half of it spills,
They rustle in laughter, forgiving my ills.

Potted confessions, whispers in green,
"Last week, I was wild, now I'm just clean!"
In their leafy embrace, I find my own grace,
With ferns in my family, I've found my place!

So here's to the chaos, the joy, and the glee,
To ferns with their antics, always quirky and free.
In this home where laughter and leaves intertwine,
We bloom in our chaos, with love we all shine!

Roots of Affection

In the corner stands my fern,
Ignoring my love is his concern.
I talk to him, he just stares back,
Judging my watering, what does he lack?

My cactus grins, all spines and pride,
No need for water, what a ride!
While I'm drenched, like a wet sock,
He receives sunshine, stock after stock.

The pothos drapes, dramatic flair,
Chasing the sunlight, without a care.
I trip on leaves that cascade wide,
In my home, is it me who hides?

Roots are tangled, hearts rewind,
In this jungle, we're quite entwined.
They may be plants, but they know best,
My love grows strong, a leafy jest.

Growing Loves in Little Pots

In tiny pots, my hopes take flight,
Each sprout a dream, oh what a sight!
But one rogue bean went rogue and sprouted,
A vine invasion, my plans shouted!

Watering can in hand, I sing,
Making up songs that make me swing.
Each time I spill, they seem to grin,
Ah yes, that's how my day begins!

My herbs compete for kitchen space,
Basil, mint, they all share my place.
While I chop, they grow quite proud,
Marking their territory, so loud!

With every leaf, a giggle too,
Who knew plants could have this view?
In my garden, full of cheer,
Love blooms bright, let's all draw near!

Whispering Leaves and Silent Growth

The succulents whisper, 'Just relax!'
While I overwater like a clumsy tax.
Their silence speaks in tiny forms,
While I juggle care in all my norms.

A spider plant's long legs do sway,
Dancing alone, as I work away.
Are they laughing or just quite chill?
Their secret life, gives me a thrill!

Each leaf a journal, stories spun,
Of sunlight moments and water fun.
They grow up tall, while I just sit,
Laughing at their antics, never quit!

As I prune, they tease with glee,
Is it me or is it them, I see?
In this dance of green and light,
We share a laugh, oh what a sight!

Beneath the Canopy of Care

Underneath my leafy throne,
Lies a garden where love is grown.
Each petal tells of a goofy tale,
Of sunny days and the oddest fail.

I spy on weeds, quite the cheeky crew,
Plotting to take my love from view.
But armed with gloves, I make my stand,
They underestimate this plant-filled land!

A rubber tree with a rubber grin,
"Water less!" it shouts, my daily sin.
Yet still I water, I simply must,
For love like this, it's a sacred trust.

Growing green and giggles, bask in cheer,
In this home, all feel welcome here.
With every sprout, new laughter sprouts,
In this jungle, I'm the one who doubts!

Ferns and Family: Our Story

In the corner grows a fern,
It leans to see, it's quite the turn.
Each morning, I swear, it stares at me,
Judging my coffee with glee.

My cat thinks it's a jungle gym,
Climbing up, on a whimsical whim.
I chase him off with a playful shout,
He gives me a look, is he out or about?

Pots of green, they live and sway,
Bouncing to music, they frolic and play.
A spritz of water, their dance gets grand,
They thrive on my love, and sometimes, a hand.

At family dinners, they join the fun,
A leafy audience, second to none.
Their gossip's loud when lights go low,
With secrets of sunlight, they steal the show.

Petals of Promise

A flower bloomed with a cheeky grin,
Beside it, a bug, a bass player within.
They jam all night, to a symphony sweet,
While I trip over pots, quite the feat!

My daisies debate which color's the best,
They're stuck in their roots, but still they jest.
Sunflowers laugh, and tease the rest,
Who knew gardening could be such a quest?

Now I water dreams with a splash and a wink,
Planting wild thoughts, more than you think.
Each bloom holds a story, a giggle inside,
In petals of promise, my hopes take pride.

I dance with the beat of the buzzing bees,
They swarm like my family, all busy with ease.
In my garden of laughter, we pour out our hearts,
With nature as witness, a good love departs.

Nurtured by Nature

I whispered sweet nothings to my stubborn sprout,
It sighed like a teen, wanting to pout.
"Grow, little friend!" I coax, puffing air,
While it droops in protest, unaware of my care.

The soil comes alive with worms that chat,
They gossip about me, and my green pet cat.
"Not that plant again!" they wiggle and squirm,
Just one more reason I laugh at the term.

Leaves have personalities, I swear it's true,
Some dance in the light, while others just stew.
Each pot a character, a story to share,
In my green little world, there's laughter to spare.

With every bloom, there's a tale to unfold,
Of roots and of petals, of young and of old.
So in this green venture, I find much delight,
Nurtured by nature, our hearts feel just right.

Sprouts of Joy in Every Corner

In every nook, a sprout does peek,
Winking at me, it's playing hide and seek.
I tiptoe in hopes to catch them all,
But they giggle and bounce, never to fall.

Lavender scents weave through the air,
While my herbs conspire without a care.
Mint's making mojitos, while basil's the chef,
In this garden party, we laugh quite a heft!

Oh, the joys of plants, it's a leafy affair,
With cacti that tease and flowers that dare.
Each morning I rise, to their happy faces,
Like tiny green friends in our cozy places.

So here's to the sprouts that bring us delight,
In pots and in hearts, they shimmer so bright.
With nature as joy, our laughter's not thin,
In every corner, let the fun begin!

Pruning Doubts

Snip, snip, the shears in hand,
Might I kill my friend, oh man!
Leaves fall like confetti around,
Was this the choice I wanted found?

A wilted leaf talks back to me,
You're not quite the gardener, you see.
I turn around, and there they glare,
Judgment from plants, they don't play fair!

Still, I chop with clueless glee,
Through trial, error, we'll agree.
It's just a phase, this plant and me,
Next week, we'll be a sight to see!

In the flowers' gaze, I find my muse,
Maybe not all is lost, just some blues.
With every snip, my doubts take flight,
Pruning doubts? Nah, more like delight!

Growing Hope

In my window, a seedling peeks,
Promises of green, a future it seeks.
Watered with care and a dash of fate,
I watch it sprout, my new bestmate.

Tiny leaves stretching towards the sun,
Together we bask in the rays, oh fun!
A spritz here, a pinch of soil there,
My plant believes, and so do I, I swear!

Dancing pot, oh how you sway,
With every gust, you brighten my day.
Your roots are tangled, but I don't mind,
In our garden magic, hope's what we find.

Grow, little friend, don't take too long,
With every inch, you sing your song.
A pot of joy, my hopes took flight,
Growing together, what a silly sight!

Roots of Togetherness

Side by side, our pots do share,
Entangled roots, a silly affair.
Dirt on my hands, oh, what a mess,
But in this chaos, we find success.

A dash of fertilizer, a little wink,
Why do they smell? I'll hardly think!
With little vines creeping all around,
In this jungle, true love is found.

Water fights break out—oops, my bad!
Joy in every splash makes me glad.
Who'd thought bonding could be so sweet,
In this green treat, life's no defeat!

Together we grow, through thick and thin,
With every leaf, the laughter begins.
Roots intertwined, let's never part,
In this wild garden, you hold my heart!

A Symphony of Growing Things

In the corner, a trumpet flower plays,
While my leafy friends join in the fray.
With each note that wafts through the air,
We dance with petals, a jazzy affair.

Potted herbs in chorus sing,
Mint and basil, the songs they bring.
Chives sway gently, thymes join the band,
A whimsical melody, oh so grand!

Sunlight beams, a spotlight above,
I'll hum along, my plants I love.
With laughter and giggles, we sway in tune,
Growing together, under the moon.

Nature's concert, the soil our stage,
Life's hilarious play, at every age.
In this symphony, we're never alone,
With foliage friends, we've truly grown!

Heartfelt Harvests

Tiny tomatoes hang with pride,
I squeal in joy, can't let this slide.
Tasted one fresh, burst of delight,
A garden feast, oh, what a sight!

Carrots peek, their tops on display,
Who knew veggies could brighten my day?
A harvest party, cheerfully lived,
Feeling like I've truly achieved!

Basil's aroma adds spice to the air,
Cooked with laughter, none can compare.
Chop, chop, cooking with plants feels right,
With every bite, a giggle takes flight!

Bountiful garden, you're such a tease,
Heartfelt harvests, my love's sure to please.
With every slice, joy multiplies,
Laughter and feasting under blue skies!

Soil and Soul Connections

In the dirt I dig for joy,
Finding roots like a little boy.
Worms wiggle in a dance of glee,
I wonder if they laugh at me.

Potted plants all in a row,
Staring blankly, putting on a show.
Talk to me! Don't be so shy,
I promise not to let you die!

Water spills like a bad perfume,
I swear it's a plant's evil tune.
They stretch and lean in every light,
Looking for sun with all their might.

Fertilizer, oh what a gift,
Makes the plants do a little lift.
But when I spill it on my shoes,
It's my feet that sing the blues!

Adventures in Green

Yesterday I gave a sprout a name,
"Sir Grow-a-lot", it's quite the game.
Chasing bugs with a mighty spray,
While my neighbor laughs all day.

I bought a fern, it's like a pet,
But it hasn't learned the tricks just yet.
Every day it plays a prank,
Turning brown, it's in the tank!

Cactus pride, oh so spiky,
Hugging it would be quite dicey.
Yet with needles, it stands so tall,
What's the secret? I want it all!

Kitchen herbs, they sprout and shout,
Basil whispers, "Make a route."
But when I chop them for my stew,
They plead, "Hey, this isn't cool!"

The Languages of Leaves

Whispering leaves in the evening light,
Sharing secrets, what a delight!
They gossip 'bout the pests they see,
While I sip my herbal tea.

A leaf quivers, it's on the brink,
Telling tales of soil and stink.
Are they plotting a great escape?
Or just dreaming of a better shape?

I tried to teach them how to dance,
But they just wobbled; no second chance.
With every sway, I felt so bold,
And yet, I'm still a sight to behold.

Their chatter fills the sunny air,
Each petal knows the games we share.
In leafy tongues, I hear my name,
A funny world, but still the same!

Tales from the Greenhouse

In the greenhouse, a raucous crew,
Where each plant claims a debonair view.
Tomatoes gossip, cucumbers sigh,
While I try to grow, oh my, oh my!

A sunflower towers, calls out my name,
"Hey, little human! You're playing a game!"
While ferns sway as if in the know,
What's their secret? I wish I could go!

My orchids boast with a floral grin,
But I drop them once, and they spin!
"You think you're fancy, look at the dirt,"
I'd laugh, but I'm the one in the hurt.

Amidst the pots, chaos ensues,
Plant battles break out, who to choose?
Yet at day's end, with love we part,
Each silly tale stays close to my heart.

Leafy Lessons

In the morning light, I water with glee,
A jungle of greens, they're thriving for me.
But one little sprout, so eager to rise,
Decided to flop, oh what a surprise!

Fertilizer fiasco, what did I choose?
Plant food or cake? No wonder they bruise!
My leafy companions, a motley crew,
Dancing and swaying, they're always askew.

Cactus thinks he's tough, a prickly chap,
While ferns go all droopy, taking a nap.
But oh the advice, they whisper to me,
"Just laugh it off, and stick to the tea!"

Each tiny leaf holds a lesson to learn,
In this green little world, my heart starts to churn.
With humor and soil, I cherish it all,
For in these green moments, I always stand tall.

From Soil to Soul

With dirt on my hands, I pot with delight,
Hoping this seedling will sprout up just right.
But lo and behold, it makes quite the mess,
Soil on my shirt? Oh, what a distress!

I named my philodendron Phil, sweet and bold,
But talked to him too much, his leaves turned to gold.
"Are you a statue?" my friends would jest,
But Phil just looked happy, enjoying the jest.

I tried to keep calm, I tried to be cool,
Yet Lavender kept wilting, breaking the rule.
"Just give me a break!" she seemed to declare,
"I'm not here for drama, just a breath of fresh air!"

From soil to soul, these plants teach me cheer,
They never care, just grow year after year.
Through laughter and toil, we'll weather the storm,
In this quirk of a garden, my heart feels warm.

Embracing the Green

Oh how they beckon, my leafy delight,
Each day I nurture, in morning's soft light.
Yet one little sprout, with a will of its own,
Decided to dance like it was on loan!

My hangers-on friends, they're quite in a mood,
Some shyly blossom, while others get rude.
"Not another selfie!" the succulents shout,
While ferns roll their eyes, still frozen in doubt.

With nature's own charm, they keep me afloat,
Even when mishaps make me want to gloat.
One very fine morning, I stepped on a pot,
Now I wear clay shoes—oh, what a thought!

Embracing the green, a colorful mess,
Every little leaf adds to my happiness.
So here's to my plants, my goofy crew,
In a world full of laughter, they blossom anew!

Of Pots and Heartstrings

In pots stacked high, a colorful sight,
Some plants tell stories, others start fights.
With basil a diva, and mint huffing air,
Each day in the garden feels like a fair!

The rubber plant's tough, stands up to the test,
While spider plants dangle, just doing their best.
"Oh good grief," I say, "stop fighting for space!"
Yet they tease and tangle, with grace and with pace.

Who knew I'd find solace, not just a chore,
As roots intertwined, they opened a door.
With each little bloom, I'm laughing aloud,
Plants as my pals, I'm no longer cowed!

Of pots and heartstrings, it's a bright little play,
In a garden of mischief, I'm here to stay.
With funny little moments, we grow hand in hand,
In this verdant paradise, oh isn't life grand!

Healing with Heliconia

In a jungle of green, I found my muse,
Heliconia swayed, refusing to lose.
It waved its petals, so bright and bold,
Claiming it's therapy, or so I'm told.

With water and sun, it drinks in delight,
Yet here I am, losing the watering fight.
It whispers sweet nothings, never a care,
While I trip on my own, gasping for air!

They say it's all zen, a calming spree,
But my friend just wilted, oh, woe is me!
Each leaf a reminder, to keep on my toes,
Healing is messy, as everyone knows.

Embracing the Earth

Digging the soil, I'm feeling quite grand,
But my hands are now caked, I need a new plan.
A shovel in hand, earth flinging like mud,
Yet here I stand, a proud soil-bearer stud.

I plant in a frenzy, like I'm on a spree,
But weeds are the uninvited guests, can't you see?
With roots everywhere, they laugh and they tease,
While I fight their chaos, praying for ease.

Embracing my fate, amidst dirt and delight,
I ponder if I'm doing this gardening right.
My garden's a riddle, a wild, wacky dream,
But hey, it grows, or so it would seem!

The Secrets of Sprouts

I bought a seed pack, tucked it away,
Hoping for miracles, oh what a grand play!
I watered with love and whispered sweet vows,
Yet sprout came a slug, now eating my plows!

My patience unraveling, I've become a mess,
Those little green thugs, I must confess.
While waiting for growth, I chant and I scheme,
But the seedlings just giggle, living the dream.

With tips from a friend who swears they know best,
I followed their guide, put my knowledge to test.
But they've turned into weeds, oh what a surprise,
The secrets of sprouts are a clever disguise!

Blooming Emotions

In my sunny nook, I watch blossoms sway,
They bloom with such flair, like they're on Broadway.
But here comes the bee, buzzing loud in delight,
While I run for cover, it's quite the fright!

I talk to my flowers, share secrets and dreams,
Though they'd likely ignore all my worldly schemes.
Still, they listen intently, with petals unfurled,
Oh, the blooming emotions that life has whirled.

They sway with my laughter, they bob with my sighs,
Each color's a tale, beneath sunny skies.
With petals as witnesses, singing their part,
Blooming emotions, oh, they fill up my heart!

Petals of Parenthood

Watering cans scattered everywhere,
So many plants, I hope they share!
Each sprout a child, I tend with care,
Why do they grow with such a flair?

Fertilizer smells like pizza night,
I question if I've got this right.
Talking to leaves feels quite polite,
But does it count if they take flight?

Sunshine hugs them every day,
While I chase pests that want to play.
My leafy kids, they make me sway,
Oh, how they make me laugh and stay!

So here I am, a parent proud,
Talking to veggies, singing loud.
With every leaf, I feel unbowed,
In this crazy, green-filled crowd.

Cultivated Comfort

My cacti throw the fiercest looks,
Do they know they're in my books?
Can't touch them, or I'll lose my hooks,
Yet their sharp humor always cooks.

Succulents line the windowsill,
Promising me they won't spill.
But once a week, they test my will,
Remind me rain's a skill to drill.

In pots they giggle, grow and twirl,
Some dance like there's a greenish whirl.
I swear, they've just begun a curl,
As I nurse a root that might unfurl.

Oh, the joy of leafy cheer,
Each empty pot fills up with beer!
Wait, that's just water, let me steer,
Life in dirt is truly dear.

A Gardener's Heartbeat

My heart beats with the rhythms of green,
Each sprout a dream, each weed a glean.
Why does the soil smell so obscene?
Yet in this garden, I feel like a queen.

Mismatched pots line my sunny pad,
I talk to plants, but it's not so bad.
Their leaves respond, though I feel mad,
Do they whisper secrets of the clad?

Every bloom brings a giggle and glee,
As petals dance like they're wild and free.
In this green craze, it's just them and me,
A world where joy grows equally.

So here I stand, mud on my shoes,
Playing with plants, I've nothing to lose.
Together we thrive, shake off the blues,
In this garden, I'll always refuse!

Seasons of Green

Springtime sprouts, a sight to see,
Each flower winks back at me.
A parade of greens, a jubilant spree,
    Who needs a garden party?

Summer sun ignites the leaves,
As I swat the bugs like thieves.
But come to think, it's still a breeze,
A comedy show in between these eves.

Fall brings colors bold and bright,
My harvest dance brings pure delight.
But then the raindrops give me fright,
As I dash and save my plants from blight.

Winter wraps them in cozy dreams,
While I sip cocoa and plot their schemes.
In this green life, or so it seems,
Laughter's the heart of all my themes.

The Tender Touch of Green Thumb

In a world of potted delight,
I water plants as day turns night.
They thrive on neglect, or so I'm told,
Yet my fingers somehow turn them cold.

Fertilizer spills on my new dress,
As I clean my mess, I still digress.
Each leafy friend needs a hug or two,
But I wonder if they know what to do.

Cacti poke me when I try to pet,
I laugh at my love, there's no regret.
Succulents smiling, all green and wise,
Yet die if they see the skies.

Oh, the tales of plants I can spin,
With each daisy, I find a win.
In my jungle, full of cheer,
I'm a funny gardener, it's crystal clear.

Tiny Hands, Big Hearts

With tiny hands, my kids approach,
Each little sprout—an eager coach.
"Is it time to water?" they ask with glee,
As mud flies high, oh woe is me!

The bucket spills, a joyful flood,
Their laughter mixes with the mud.
Planting seeds, what a magical feat,
We grow a jungle, oh what a treat!

They hug the ferns with all their might,
Chasing butterflies, a silly sight.
Leaves quiver under tiny touch,
Nature's giggles, can't thank them much.

In beats of joy, our hearts align,
Growing greens while sipping on wine.
With tiny hands, they leave their mark,
Planting love, igniting a spark.

Every Leaf a Memory

Each leaf whispers tales of my blunder,
Of days I forgot, oh what a wonder!
My rubber plant has seen my tears,
As I blame it for all my fears.

I pruned it back with reckless cheer,
And now it's sad; I shed a tear.
Every brown tip tells a story,
Of glory once bright, now lacking glory.

Sunny days bring moments of joy,
Yet I overwater like a child with a toy.
"What did I do?" I cry in despair,
Plants hold memories, I'm well aware.

But they forgive, oh how they bloom,
In every green room, there's life, there's room.
With every leaf, a chuckle or two,
My little garden, it's all about you.

Sowing Seeds of Connection

With every seed that finds its place,
I sow my hopes with a smiling face.
"Let's grow a forest!" I cheerfully shout,
But weeds appear, leaving me in doubt.

In the chaos of green, I roam about,
And in dark corners, weeds lurk, no doubt.
But even with trouble, I can't complain,
Nature's giggles wash away the pain.

Friends come over, how they laugh,
At my brown-thumbed, goofy craft.
We bond through blooms and silly chat,
Sowing seeds of laughter, imagine that!

In this garden of quirks, we cultivate joy,
A sanctuary for each girl and boy.
With every pot, I connect more,
In the sitcom of life, plants steal the floor.

The Art of Plant Parenthood

I bought a fern, it looked so bright,
Three weeks later, it lost the fight.
My friends all laughed when I confessed,
I guess I'm just not plant-obsessed.

A cactus here, a succulent there,
They promised me they'd thrive with care.
But in my home, they seem to pout,
What's wrong with me? I scream and shout.

I water them like they need a bath,
But they just wither, oh what a path!
Should I play music or offer tea?
Can plants and I ever agree?

Yet every little sprout I see,
Brings a giggle, a touch of glee.
Though I may fail in the plant game,
I'll always cherish their leafy fame.

Budding Friendships

I met a friend who knows her greens,
She shares her tips, if you know what I mean.
"Leave the light on!" she constantly said,
While I forget to water mine instead.

We started swapping little cuts,
I gave her weeds, she gave me buds.
Our plants are thriving, the laughter so bright,
Together we bloom, it feels so right.

"Your jade is fine," she'd often tease,
But mine looks more like a wilted cheese.
We joke and laugh, as friends should do,
In this garden of chaos, we've both grown too.

Sometimes I mutter, "Why do they mope?"
She just grins, "Put them in sunlight, hope!"
In this journey of pots, dirt, and light,
We bond over plants, and it feels just right.

Chronicles of Chlorophyll

Once found a plant with glorious leaves,
Placed it by the window, or so it believes.
It curled right up and turned to brown,
I thought plants loved to go to town!

My friend said, "Water it only a lot!"
Now it's soggy, looks like a spot.
With every mishap, I take a note,
Who knew plant care was such a joke?

I pruned a stem, it looked so cute,
But now it's a stick — oh what a hoot!
The stories we share about our green friends,
Are filled with giggles, never ends.

In this wilderness of class and flair,
We each have tales of plant despair.
But we keep trying, with laughter and love,
Guided by our green friends from above.

Nature's Gentle Embrace

In my living room, plants all around,
With their leafy arms, they abound.
One's leaning in for a big old hug,
While I stand back, feeling snug as a bug.

The spider plant dances to my song,
"Sing to me!" it seems to prolong.
But as I belt out my best tune,
It stares back like, "Really? Don't ruin this afternoon!"

I talk to my plants, it's quite a spree,
"Grow tall!" I shout, like a plant jubilee.
They droop and pout, I start to fret,
Maybe it's me, filled with regret.

Yet every Sunday, we host our meet,
My leafy clan and I, oh what a treat.
In this green embrace, we all find cheer,
A laugh anew, with each passing year.

www.ingramcontent.com/pod-product-compliance
Lightning Source LLC
Chambersburg PA
CBHW070315120526
44590CB00017B/2686